ANIMAL RHYME TIME!

RHYME TIME WITH ELEPHANTS!

BY JONAS EDWARDS

Gareth Stevens
PUBLISHING

Please visit our website, www.garethstevens.com. For a free color catalog of all our high-quality books, call toll free 1-800-542-2595 or fax 1-877-542-2596.

Library of Congress Cataloging-in-Publication Data

Names: Edwards, Jonas, author.
Title: Rhyme time with elephants! / Jonas Edwards.
Description: New York : Gareth Stevens Publishing, [2021] | Series: Animal rhyme time! | Includes index.
Identifiers: LCCN 2019060212 | ISBN 9781538256046 (library binding) | ISBN 9781538256022 (paperback) | ISBN 9781538256039 (6 Pack) | ISBN 9781538256053 (ebook)
Subjects: LCSH: Elephants–Juvenile literature. | Rhyme–Juvenile literature.
Classification: LCC QL737.P98 E3625 2021 | DDC 599.67–dc23
LC record available at https://lccn.loc.gov/2019060212

First Edition

Published in 2021 by
Gareth Stevens Publishing
111 East 14th Street, Suite 349
New York, NY 10003

Copyright © 2021 Gareth Stevens Publishing

Editor: Kate Mikoley

Photo credits: Cover, p. 1 Donovan van Staden/Shutterstock.com; cover, pp. 3–24 (music notes) StockSmartStart/Shutterstock.com; p. 5 John M Lund Photography Inc/DigitalVision/Getty Images; p. 7 danilovi/E+/Getty Images; p. 9 Q-lieb-in/Shutterstock.com; p. 11 Bene_A/Shutterstock.com; p. 13 John Warburton-Lee/AWL Images / Getty Images Plus; p. 15 Andrzej Kubik/Shutterstock.com; p. 17 Gallo Images - Michael Poliza/ Riser / Getty Images Plus; p. 19 Art Wolfe/ The Image Bank / Getty Images Plus; p. 21 Cheryl Ramalho/ iStock / Getty Images Plus.

All rights reserved. No part of this book may be reproduced in any form without permission in writing from the publisher, except by a reviewer.

Printed in the United States of America

Some of the images in this book illustrate individuals who are models. The depictions do not imply actual situations or events.

CPSIA compliance information: Batch #CS20GS: For further information contact Gareth Stevens, New York, New York at 1-800-542-2595.

Find us on

CONTENTS

Largest on Land.......................... 4
Home for Elephants..................... 6
Spray It!.................................... 8
Standing Tall............................. 10
Trunks and Tusks....................... 12
Active Animals.......................... 14
Amazing Mammals..................... 16
Elephant Language..................... 18
Excellent Elephants.................... 20
Glossary................................... 22
For More Information................. 23
Index....................................... 24

Boldface words appear in the glossary.

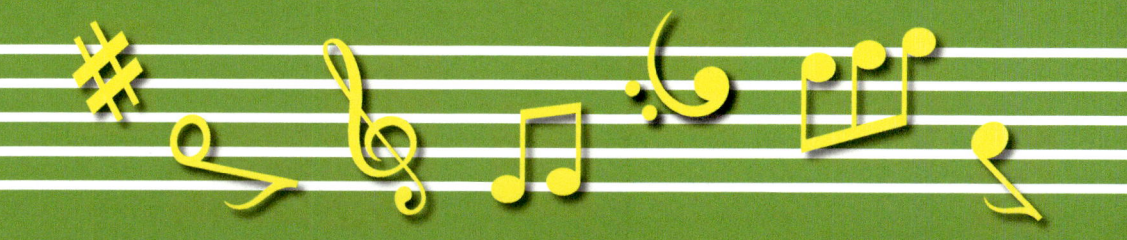

Largest on Land

Do you know the largest animals on land?

Here's a hint. Their skin is gray and their trunk is grand.

Elephants, yes! Learn more about these creatures.

Read on to find out about their homes, size, and features.

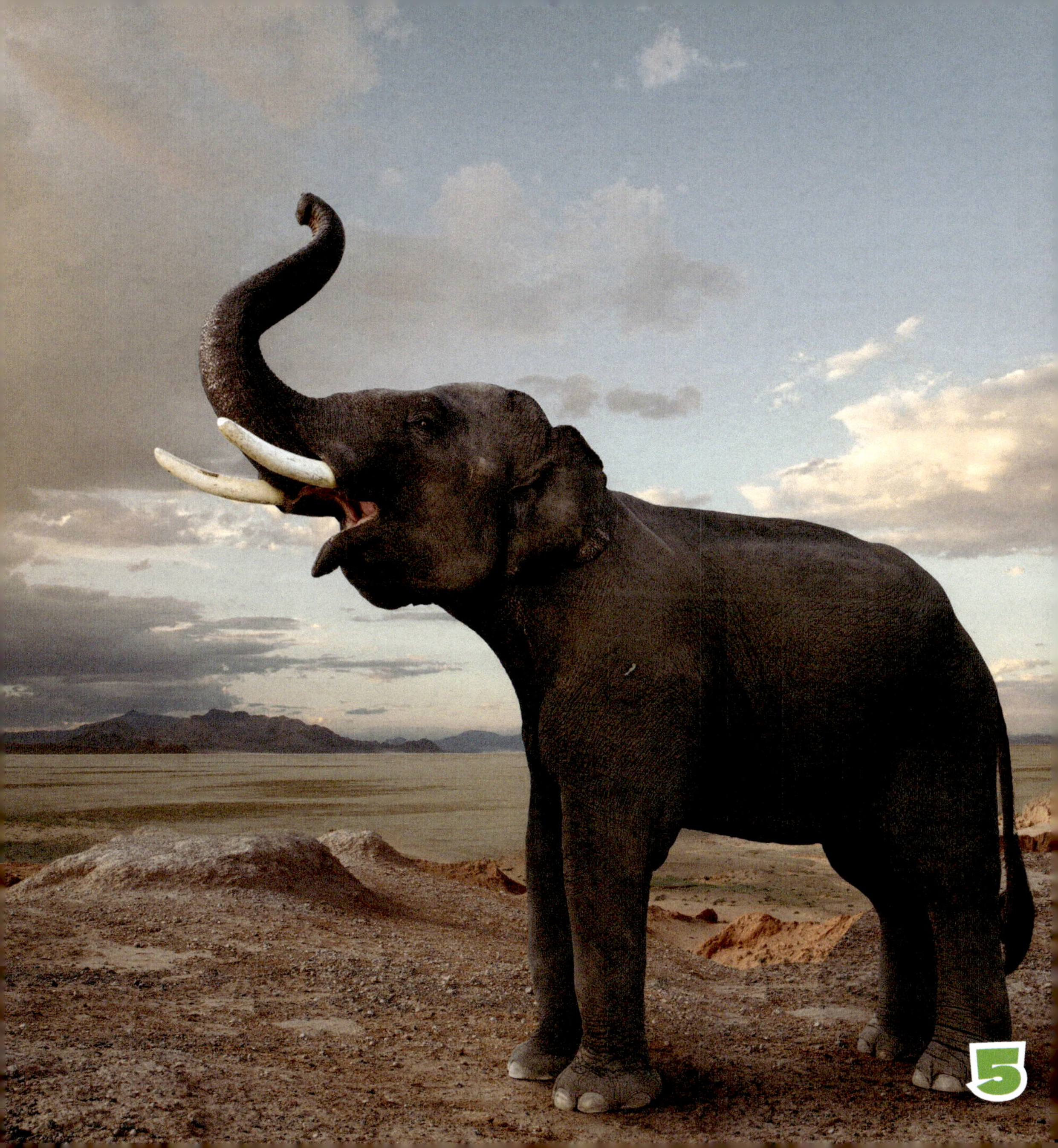

Home for Elephants

You may have seen an elephant at the zoo.

In nature, they live in **savannas**, forests, and deserts too.

An elephant may call Africa or Asia home.

When they need food or water, it's time to **roam**.

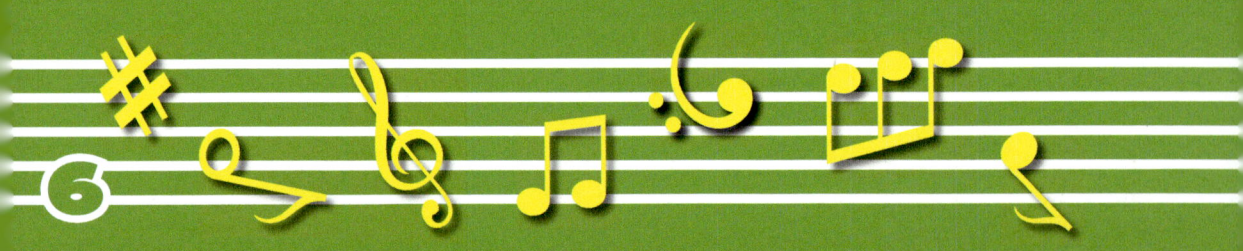

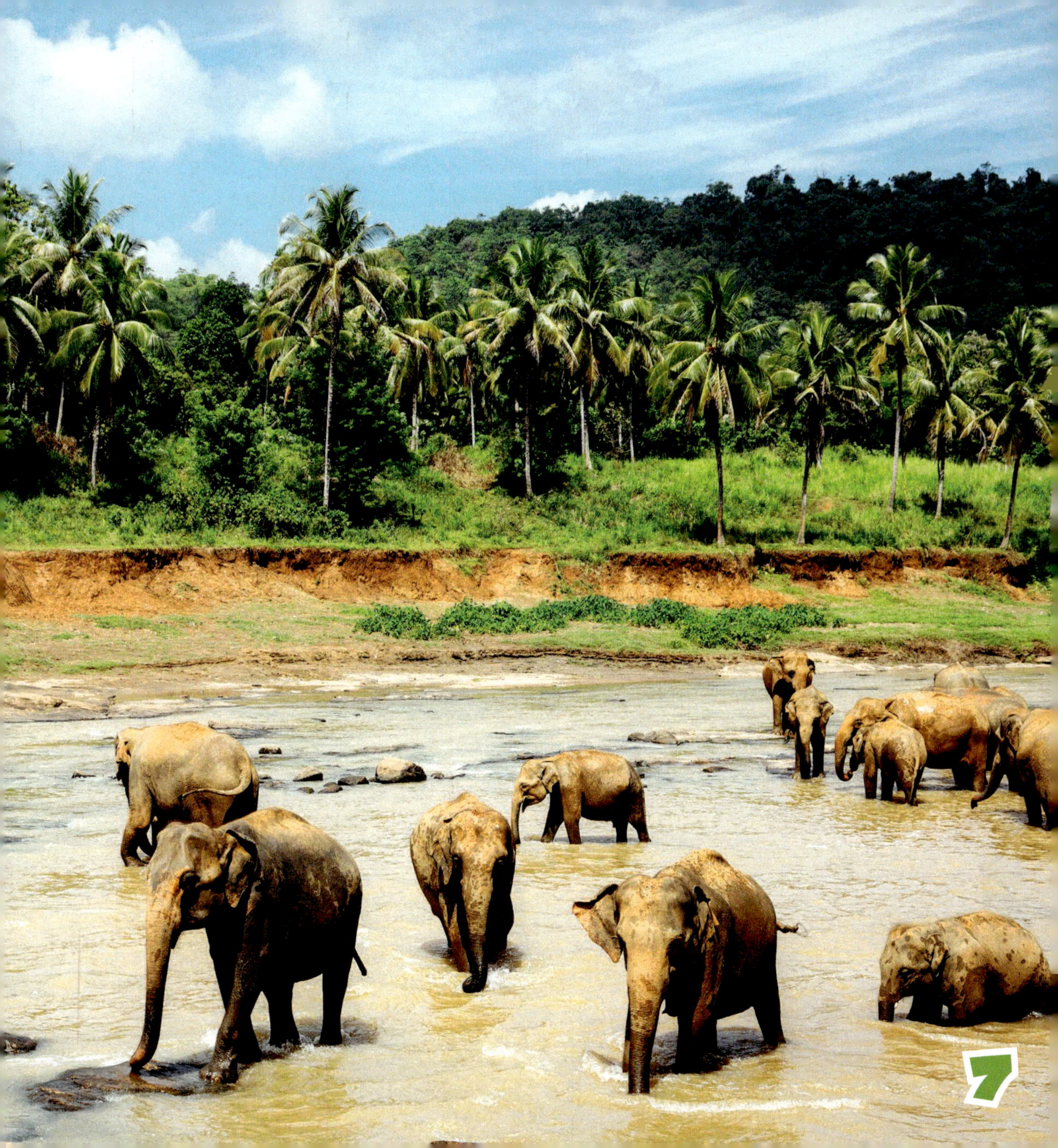

Spray It!

Elephants have a long trunk and big ears.

In the wild, they can live up to 60 years.

An elephant's trunk is really its nose!

It's used to drink, smell, and spray water like a **hose**!

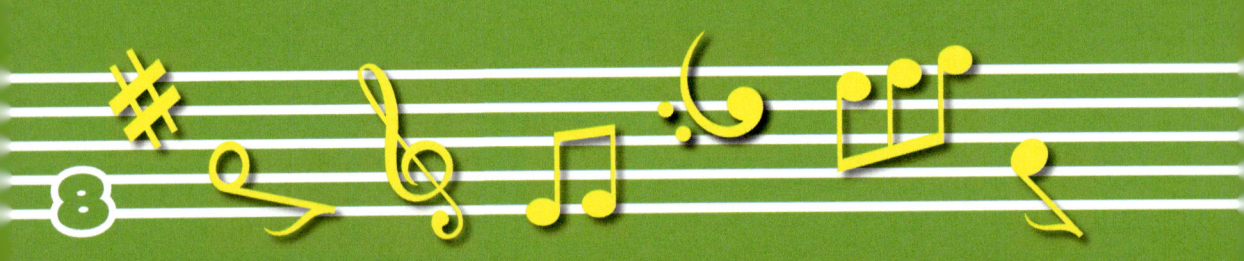

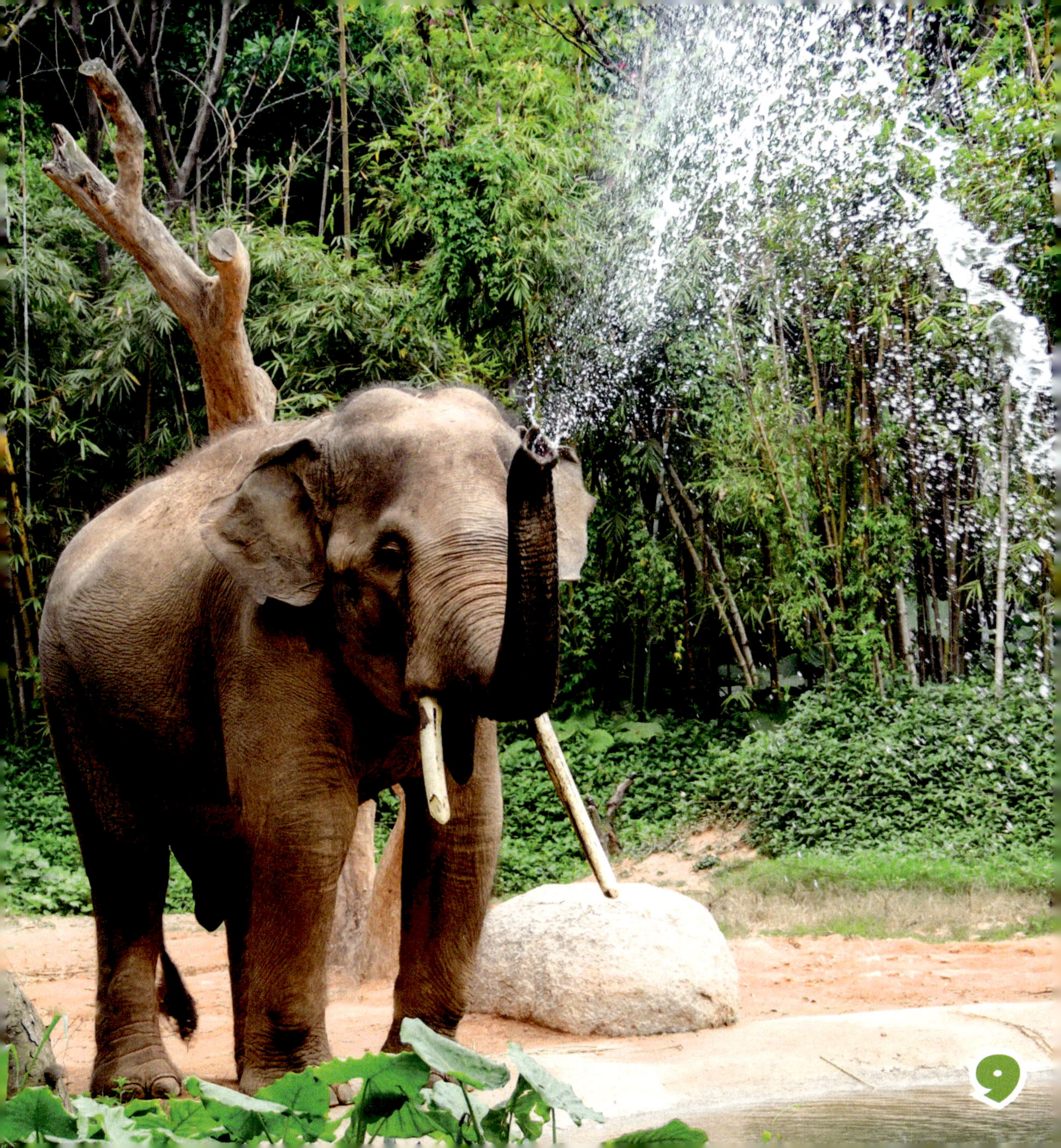

Standing Tall

Elephants use their ears to stay cool in the heat.

Grass, fruit, and leaves are a few things that they eat.

Some elephants are as tall as a bus! For animals that big, eating lots of food is a must.

11

Trunks and Tusks

An elephant's trunk has thousands of **muscles**.

It can be used to grab things and make treetops **rustle**.

The tusks are used to dig and to fight. These big teeth are made of **ivory** and are white.

TUSKS

Active Animals

Elephants bathe in mud to stay safe from the sun.

These social animals like to play and have fun!

They're known to have good memories and be smart.

Some can **recognize** themselves in mirrors and be taught to make art.

15

Amazing Mammals

Elephants are mammals. They're warm-blooded and breathe air.
These animals also feed milk to their young, have backbones, and hair.
Young elephants are commonly raised by their mothers.
Older males often go off and leave the others.

17

Elephant Language

Elephants live in groups called herds. They can **communicate**, but they don't use words.

They make sounds, like loud roars and cries.

Other elephants can hear, even if they're not nearby.

19

Excellent Elephants

Now you know how great elephants are.

Living in nature, they travel wide and they travel far.

These great big animals are smart and are strong.

If we don't care for them, they won't be around for long.

21

GLOSSARY

communicate: to share thoughts or feelings by sound, movement, or writing

hose: a long tube that liquid, such as water, can flow through

ivory: a hard, white matter that makes up the tusks of elephants and other animals

muscle: one of the parts of the body that allow movement

recognize: to know and remember something from seeing it before

roam: to wander

rustle: to make a soft, light sound by making parts of something brush against each other

savanna: a grassland with scattered patches of trees

FOR MORE INFORMATION

BOOKS

Adams, Avery. *Elephants Work Together.* New York, NY: PowerKids Press, 2018.

Murray, Julie. *Elephants.* Minneapolis, MN: Abdo Publishing, 2020.

Schuh, Mari. *The Supersmart Elephant.* Minneapolis, MN: Lerner Publications, 2019.

WEBSITES

African Elephant
kids.nationalgeographic.com/animals/mammals/african-elephant/
Check out this page to learn all about African elephants.

Are All Elephants the Same?
www.wonderopolis.org/wonder/are-all-elephants-the-same
Learn more about the different kinds of elephants around the world.

Elephants
www.dkfindout.com/us/animals-and-nature/elephants
Find more fun facts about elephants here.

Publisher's note to educators and parents: Our editors have carefully reviewed these websites to ensure that they are suitable for students. Many websites change frequently, however, and we cannot guarantee that a site's future contents will continue to meet our high standards of quality and educational value. Be advised that students should be closely supervised whenever they access the internet.

INDEX

Africa 6
Asia 6
desert 6
ears 8, 10
food 6, 10
forest 6
herd 18
ivory 12
mammal 16
muscle 12
savanna 6
size 4, 10

skin 4
smart 14, 20
sound 18
strong 20
trunk 4, 8, 12
tusks 12, 13